TEMPTING
CHICKEN
COOKBOOK

Recipes with an international
flavour for all occasions.

KÖNEMANN

WHOLE CHICKEN		
Small	1-1.25 kg	2-3 portions
Medium	1.5-1.75 kg	3-4 portions
Large	2-2.5 kg	4-5 portions
CHICKEN PIECES		
1 whole breast		1 portion
1-2 half breasts		1 portion
1-2 drumsticks (legs)		1 portion
1-2 thighs		1 portion
1 drumstick and thigh (Maryland)		1 portion
1 whole fillet (boned breast)		1 portion
1-2 half fillets (boned ½ breast)		1 portion
2 thigh fillets (boned thighs)		1 portion
3-4 chicken wings		1 portion
COOKED CHICKEN MEAT (DICED)		
1 medium chicken		about 4 cups
2 whole breasts		about 2 cups
1 thigh and drumstick		about 1 cup
Allow ½-¾ cup diced meat for each serving, depending on the recipe and other factors.		

N ot so long ago, chicken was reserved for special occasions. Only 40 years ago, a person would eat a mere four chickens a year; now, each of us is consuming about 17. Today, we think little of buying a chicken to cook for dinner, regardless of whether there's any celebrating to be done! Supermarkets and specialty chicken shops now stock ready-jointed portions – thighs, breasts, wings, drumsticks – which make meal preparation quicker and easier than ever before. You can also buy ready-cooked, barbecued chickens as well as smoked chicken.

Apart from its taste attributes, chicken is a nutritious food which is high in protein, phosphorus and niacin, and also a good source of iron. The breast is the section with the lowest fat content; in these cholesterol and diet-conscious times, it is best to trim chicken of its skin and as much fat as possible.

All food should be handled and stored carefully to avoid food poisoning, but chicken requires extreme care. Fresh, uncooked chicken should be stored in the coldest part of the refrigerator for one or two days only; make sure it is not in a position where it can drip on other foodstuffs, causing cross-contamination. Keep poultry away from strong-smelling items. Frozen chickens or chicken portions must be fully defrosted in the refrigerator

before cooking. Never leave them to defrost in the kitchen; harmful bacteria will multiply at a great rate in a warm atmosphere. Frozen poultry must be brought home from the shop as quickly as possible and stored in the freezer only if it is still rock hard. If it has begun to defrost, you must defrost it fully in the refrigerator, cook it and then freeze it.

After chopping raw chicken flesh, wash your work surfaces and utensils in very hot water, paying particular attention to chopping boards; small portions

of meat can remain in the scores made by your kitchen knives, so thorough scrubbing is important. Don't handle cooked and uncooked food together, or use the same utensils in their preparation without first washing them.

Chicken must be thoroughly cooked. Pierce the thickest part of the flesh with a knife and, if the juices run pink, continue cooking until they are clear. Cooked dishes that are not going to be eaten at once must be cooled very rapidly (immerse the base of the dish in iced water to speed things up) and placed in the refrigerator or freezer. Numerous other hints for storage and handling are given throughout this book. The recipes presented in this *Tempting Chicken Cookbook* have been inspired by the cuisines of many nations. The recipes cater for all events and time-frames.

Serving portions of chicken
Portions vary depending on:
◆ Size of chicken
◆ Method of cooking
◆ Accompanying foods
◆ Type of meal and time of day
◆ Size of serving; elderly, adult, child

METRIC POULTRY SIZES	
The size numbers for poultry are a simple indication of the weight of the bird.	
WEIGHT	SIZE
1 kg	10
1.2 kg	12
1.5 kg	15
1.8 kg	18
2 kg	20
2.5 kg	25
3 kg	30
3.5 kg	35
4 kg	40
4.5 kg	45
6 kg	60
For in-between sizes allow approximately 100 g for each number.	

Salads, soups & starters

Chicken is one of the most obliging of foods, marrying well with a wide range of flavours. For salad dishes, use dressings to coat the cooked meat. Alternatively, poach the raw meat in a combination of herbs, spices, oils and vinegars, or marinate it overnight to absorb the maximum flavour. The more inspired your choice of marinade and dressing ingredients, the more diverse your repertoire of recipes will be. Any one of the recipes in this section can be adapted to become a meal in itself. A terrine using richly flavoured chicken livers is an excellent light main course when served with a salad. Soup becomes substantial fare with a selection of breads as accompaniment.

Spicy Chicken Salad

Preparation time:
  25 minutes
Cooking time:
  Nil
Serves 6

6 chicken breast fillets
2 teaspoons olive oil
1 onion, finely chopped
2 cloves garlic, crushed
2 teaspoons curry
  powder
1 teaspoon ground
  coriander
1/2 cup mayonnaise
1/2 cup plain yoghurt
1/4 cup sultanas
2 tablespoons bottled
  French dressing

1 Place chicken breasts in a large pan with water to cover and cook gently until tender. Leave in liquid until cold.
2 Heat oil in small pan, add onion and garlic, cook, stirring, until tender. Add curry powder and coriander, stir over low heat for 1-2 minutes, cool to room temperature. Combine the onion and curry mixture with mayonnaise, yoghurt, sultanas and dressing,

Clockwise from top: Easy Chicken Vegetable Salad (page 6), Spicy Chicken Salad, Moroccan Chicken Salad (page 6)

mixing them well.
3 Shred chicken finely, combine with dressing. Serve salad with spiced rice and seasonal salad vegetables.

Easy Chicken Vegetable Salad

Preparation time:
  25 minutes + 30 minutes marinating
Cooking time:
  Nil
Serves 6

1 x 1.2 kg barbecued chicken, skinned and boned
3 carrots, peeled
250 g snow peas, strings removed
400 g can baby corn, drained
1 red capsicum, cut into small squares

Dressing
3 spring onions, finely chopped
1/4 cup white wine vinegar
2 cloves garlic, finely chopped
2 teaspoons shredded fresh ginger
1 teaspoon Dijon mustard
2/3 cup oil
1 tablespoon soy sauce
1/2 teaspoon sesame oil
freshly ground black pepper

1 Cut chicken into bite-sized strips. Place in a large bowl. Blanch carrots in boiling water for 3 minutes; drain. Rinse in cold water. Cut in thin, diagonal slices and add to chicken.
2 Blanch snow peas and corn for about 30 seconds. Halve peas diagonally; the corn lengthwise. Add to chicken with the capsicum.
3 To prepare the Dressing: Combine spring onion, vinegar, garlic, ginger and mustard. Gradually whisk in oil, soy sauce and sesame oil, seasoning to taste with pepper. Pour over salad and toss to combine.

4 Marinate at room temperature 30 minutes before serving.

Moroccan Chicken Salad

Preparation time:
  35 minutes
Cooking time:
  Nil
Serves 4

1 x 1 kg cooked chicken, skinned and boned
3 medium oranges
12 dates, stoned and halved
6 radishes, thinly sliced
1/4 cup whole blanched almonds
2 tablespoons lemon juice
2 tablespoons olive oil
1/2 teaspoon ground cinnamon
1/4 teaspoon garam masala
freshly ground pepper

1 Cut chicken into thin strips. Peel oranges, removing all pith; cut into thin slices.
2 Combine chicken, oranges, dates, radishes and almonds.
3 Whisk together lemon juice, oil, cinnamon, garam masala and pepper to taste. Pour mixture over salad ingredients, toss to combine, serve immediately.

HINT

Always remove bones and skin from cooked chicken pieces when preparing salads. Cut or shred the chicken into neat, bite-sized pieces.

Smoked Chicken Salad with Sweet and Sour Dressing

Smoked Chicken Salad with Sweet and Sour Dressing

Preparation time:
  25 minutes
Cooking time:
  Nil
Serves 4-6

1 x 150 g tub salad sprouts (see Note)
1 carrot, peeled and cut into thin strips
150 g oyster mushrooms (see Note)
150 g snow peas
1/4 cup cashews
1 x 1 kg smoked chicken, flesh removed and cut into chunks (see Note)

Dressing
1/4 cup olive oil
2 tablespoons white wine vinegar
2 tablespoons prepared sweet and sour sauce
few drops Tabasco sauce

1 Spread a layer of sprouts on a serving plate. Top with remaining ingredients.

2 To prepare Dressing: Place all ingredients in a screw-top jar. Shake well. **3** Pour over salad just before serving. Serve salad with boiled new potatoes.

Note: A combination of bean sprouts and alfalfa can be used if salad sprouts are unavailable. Ordinary mushrooms may be substituted for the oyster variety. Plain cooked chicken and smoked chicken are interchangeable in salad dishes.

7

Chicken and Corn Soup

1. For Chicken and Corn Soup: Skim off scum from stock after boiling.

2. Add chopped vegetables, peppercorns and bouquet garni to the stock.

Chicken and Corn Soup

Preparation time:
  1½ hours + overnight
  standing
Cooking time:
  12 minutes
Serves 6

Chicken Stock
*1.5-2 kg chicken bones,
  meat and giblets,
  trimmed of fat*
cold water
2 onions
2 carrots
2 stalks celery
6 peppercorns
bouquet garni (see Note)

Soup
3 cups chicken stock
*2 cups shredded,
  cooked chicken meat*
*1 x 440 g can creamed
  corn*
2 tablespoons cornflour
2 tablespoons water
*6 spring onions,
  chopped*

1 tablespoon soy sauce
1 teaspoon sesame oil
*extra spring onions,
  sliced, for garnish*

1 To prepare Chicken Stock: Place chicken and enough cold water to cover in a large pan. Slowly bring to the boil. Skim off any scum as required.
2 Chop all vegetables roughly, leaving skin on. Add to pan with peppercorns and bouquet garni. Reduce heat. Simmer, uncovered, for 1-1½ hours, adding water as required.
3 Strain stock into a large bowl, discard bones and vegetables, cool. Cover with plastic wrap. Refrigerate overnight. Discard congealed fat.
4 To prepare Chicken Soup: Bring stock to the boil in a large pan, add chicken and corn. Blend cornflour with water to

form a smooth paste, stir into stock. Simmer for 3 minutes, stir in spring onions and soy sauce.
5 Simmer for 2 minutes. Remove from heat. Stir in sesame oil. Serve garnished with extra spring onion.

Note: A bouquet garni consists of a few sprigs of parsley, a bay leaf and a teaspoon of dried thyme tied in a double thickness of muslin. Always remove bouquet garni before serving.

Chicken Soup with Dumplings

These dumplings are a combination of chicken meat and vegetables.
Preparation time:
  25 minutes
Cooking time:
  15 minutes
Serves 6

3. Strain simmered stock into a bowl and discard the bones and vegetables.

4. Blend cornflour and water and stir into the soup. Simmer for 3 minutes.

9

1 chicken breast fillet
2 eggs
½ cup finely chopped
  leek
½ cup finely chopped
  onion
½ cup finely chopped
  carrot
2 cups fresh white
  breadcrumbs
1 tablespoon chopped
  parsley
1 teaspoon pepper
1 teaspoon dried thyme
3 cups rich chicken
  stock
chopped parsley, extra

1 Cut chicken into small pieces. Place eggs in food processor, process until thick and creamy. Add leek, process until smooth, then add onion and carrot and process again until smooth. Add chicken pieces and blend until mixture has thickened and is smooth; transfer to bowl.
2 Add breadcrumbs, parsley, pepper and thyme, mix well. Shape portions between 2 large spoons dipped in cold water, place dumplings on a lightly greased, flat tray and keep covered until all are made.
3 Gently spoon dumplings into simmering chicken stock and cook until they float to the surface. Cover pan and simmer

for 10 more minutes. Divide the dumplings between 6 soup bowls and pour ½ cup chicken stock over each serving. Sprinkle with chopped parsley.

HINT
Chicken stock will keep for one week in the refrigerator and up to four months in the freezer.

Chicken Laksa

Preparation time:
  20 minutes
Cooking time:
  25 minutes
Serves 4

4 cups chicken stock
2 chicken breast fillets,
  cut into strips
125 g bean sprouts
250 g rice vermicelli
2 tablespoons oil
1 onion, finely chopped
1 clove garlic, crushed
2 fresh chillies, chopped
  (see Note)
1 teaspoon ground
  turmeric
2 teaspoons ground
  coriander
2 cups milk
1 cup coconut milk
2 spring onions, sliced

1 Bring stock to the boil in a large pan. Reduce heat, add chicken pieces. Simmer

for 5 minutes. Remove from heat, cover, allow to stand for 10 minutes.
2 Remove chicken from pan with a slotted spoon. Reserve stock. Set aside.
3 Blanch sprouts by soaking in boiling water for 30 seconds. Drain. Refresh under cold water. Set aside.
4 Place vermicelli in a large bowl. Cover with boiling water. Allow to stand for 10 minutes. Drain. Set aside.
5 Heat oil in a pan. Cook onion and garlic until tender. Add chillies, turmeric and coriander. Cook, stirring, for 30 seconds.
6 Gradually add reserved stock. Bring to the boil. Reduce heat. Stir in milk and coconut milk. Simmer, uncovered, for 15 minutes, stirring occasionally.
7 Fill each of 4 soup bowls two-thirds full with noodles. Top with equal quantities of sprouts and chicken. Pour over soup. Garnish with sliced spring onions.

Note: Rice vermicelli is available from some supermarkets and specialty Asian stores. Other types of noodle may be substituted. Dried chillies may be used in place of fresh.

Chicken Laksa and Chicken Soup with Dumplings (page 9)

Clockwise from top: Chicken San Choy Bow (page 14), Herb-marinated Chicken Wings, Warm Chicken Capsicum Salad

Herb-marinated Chicken Wings

Preparation time:
  35 minutes +
  overnight marinating
Cooking time:
  35 minutes
Makes about 24 sticks

1 kg chicken wings

Marinade
2 teaspoons finely
  grated lemon rind
1 tablespoon lemon
  juice
1/3 cup olive oil
2 tablespoons white
  wine
2 tablespoons white
  wine vinegar
3 cloves garlic,
  crushed
1 tablespoon chopped
  parsley
1 tablespoon chopped dill
freshly ground black
  pepper

1 Wash and dry
wings. Cut off wing tips
at joint. Cut wings in
two through centre
joint.
2 Holding one end of
each wing half, trim
around bone with a
sharp knife to free
meat. (Discard small
bone visible in smaller
half of wing.) Cut,
scrape and pull meat
down to large end.
3 Pull skin and meat
down over end of bone
to resemble drumsticks.
4 Combine all
marinade ingredients in
a large glass or ceramic
bowl. Add drumsticks.
Cover with plastic
wrap. Refrigerate
overnight.
5 Cook on the
barbecue or bake in a
moderate oven 180°C
for 30-35 minutes,
basting frequently.

Warm Chicken Capsicum Salad

Preparation time:
  35 minutes
Cooking time:
  Nil
Serves 4

1 small onion, thinly
  sliced
2 tablespoons olive oil
2 large capsicum,
  seeded, cut into thin
  strips
1 x 1 kg cooked
  chicken, skinned and
  cut into pieces
1 tablespoon soy sauce
1/4 teaspoon Chinese
  five-spice powder
pinch sugar
freshly ground black
  pepper
1 tablespoon vinegar
1/4 cup blanched
  almonds, toasted

1 In a pan, cook onion
in half the oil until
golden. Add capsicum
strips and cook until

crisp-tender, about 5 minutes.

2 Stir in chicken, soy sauce, five-spice powder, sugar and seasonings to taste. Heat through. Transfer to serving bowl or individual plates.

3 Combine vinegar and remaining oil; drizzle over salad. Serve garnished with almonds.

Chicken San Choy Bow

Preparation time:
  20 minutes
Cooking time:
  8 minutes
Serves 6

500 g chicken mince
125 g sliced ham, finely
  chopped
1 egg
1 tablespoon soy sauce
1 teaspoon cornflour
1 tablespoon oil
1 x 190 g can
  champignons, drained
  and chopped
1/4 cup chopped
  bamboo shoots
1 onion, finely chopped
1 teaspoon finely
  chopped fresh ginger
1 lettuce, washed and
  dried

1 Combine mince and ham. Whisk egg with soy sauce and cornflour. Stir into mince mixture.

2 Heat oil in pan or wok. Stir-fry mince mixture until chicken mince is browned, breaking up any lumps with a fork. Add champignons, bamboo shoots, onion and ginger. Cook, stirring,

for about 2 minutes.

3 To serve, spoon mince mixture into lettuce leaves. Roll up leaves and serve with a little Chinese-style plum sauce. Eat parcels with your fingers.

Chicken Liver and Brandy Pâté

Preparation time:
  30 minutes
Cooking time:
  Nil
Makes about 1 1/2 cups

125 g butter
1 large onion, chopped
2 cloves garlic, crushed
2 rashers rindless
  bacon, chopped
250 g chicken livers,
  trimmed
1/4 teaspoon dried thyme
freshly ground black
  pepper
2 tablespoons cream
1 tablespoon brandy
30 g butter extra, melted

Topping
60 g butter, melted
2 tablespoons snipped
  chives

1 Melt butter in a pan. Add onion, garlic and bacon. Cook until onion is tender and bacon is cooked.

2 Add chicken livers. Cook, stirring occasionally, for 5-10 minutes. Remove from

Chicken Liver and Brandy Pâté

heat. Stir in the remaining ingredients.

3 Spoon mixture into a food processor or blender. Process until smooth. Pour into serving dishes.

4 To prepare Topping: Pour melted butter over pâté. Sprinkle with chives. Refrigerate overnight. Serve with crackers, toast or crusty French bread.

Note: Pâté will keep in the refrigerator for up to one week, covered with plastic wrap. Most pâtés are at their best one or two days after they are made.

Chicken and Mushroom Terrine

Preparation time:
  35 minutes
Cooking time:
  1 hour
Makes 1 loaf; about 16 slices

125 g mushrooms
500 g chicken mince
250 g chicken livers
2 rashers rindless
  bacon, chopped
2 eggs
1/2 cup cream
1 tablespoon fresh
  basil, chopped
freshly ground black
  pepper
6 rashers rindless
  bacon, extra

Chicken and Mushroom Terrine

1 Process mushrooms in a food processor or blender until finely chopped. Set aside.

2 Process chicken mince, livers and bacon until well combined. Add eggs, one at a time, blending well between each addition.

3 With the motor running, slowly pour cream through chute. Pour mixture into a bowl. Stir in mushrooms, basil and seasonings.

4 Line base and sides of a 13 x 23 cm loaf tin with bacon rashers. Pour mixture into tin. Fold ends of bacon over to cover top.

5 Place in a roasting pan half filled with boiling water (see Note)

in a moderate oven 180°C for about 1 hour or until firm. Cool. Refrigerate. Unmould onto a serving platter, slice and serve with French bread or a seasonal green salad.

Note: This method of cooking is known as *bain marie*. It protects delicate mixtures from becoming overcooked and tough during long periods of cooking.

15

Family favourites

The aroma of a slow-cooking roast or a succulent chicken pie gets the tastebuds working in keen anticipation of treats to come. The exertions of the working week are soon alleviated when family members gather around the table to chat unhurriedly and savour a beautifully cooked and well-flavoured meal. Traditional recipes such as Roast Chicken with Bacon and Bread Sauce are hard to beat. And, we've drawn on some international influences - from India, South East Asia, Italy and France - to bring you family food at its best. These dishes require a little more preparation and cooking time than weekdays may allow; keep them for weekends and special occasions.

Deep-dish Chicken Pie

A tasty main course to make with leftover roast or steamed chicken. Or, buy half a cooked chicken and turn it into this treat.

Preparation time:
  30 minutes
Cooking time:
  25 minutes
Serves 4

60 g butter
1 small onion, finely
  chopped
125 g button
  mushrooms, halved
1/2 cup celery, finely
  chopped
1/4 cup plain flour
1 1/2 cups chicken stock
1/2 cup cream
2 cups chopped, cooked
  chicken, skin removed
freshly ground black
  pepper
1 sheet ready-rolled
  puff pastry
beaten egg, for glaze

1 Heat the butter in a pan and gently cook onion until soft and golden. Add mushrooms and celery and cook, stirring, for

Clockwise from top: Deep-dish Chicken Pie, Roast Chicken with Bacon and Bread Sauce (page 18), Spanish-style Chicken Casserole (page 22)

another 3-4 minutes.

2 Sprinkle flour over the vegetables and stir in. Slowly add the chicken stock and stir until sauce boils and thickens. Mix in cream and chicken and season with pepper.

3 Spoon mixture into a greased, deep, 6-cup capacity casserole or soufflé dish. Cut a circle of pastry the same size as the dish and place over filling. Decorate with leaves or little chicken shapes made from pastry trimmings, and attach to pastry lid with beaten egg. Brush top all over with beaten egg and bake in a hot oven 200°C for 20-25 minutes or until pastry is golden.

Roast Chicken with Bacon and Bread Sauce

Preparation time:
 45 minutes
Cooking time:
 1½ hours
Serves 4

1 x 1.5 kg chicken
2 large sprigs fresh
 rosemary
2 cloves garlic, peeled
15 g butter, melted
3 rashers bacon, rind
 removed
1 tablespoon oil

½ cup chicken stock
2 teaspoons fresh
 rosemary leaves, extra

Bread Sauce
1 small onion, finely
 chopped
1 cup milk
1 bay leaf
4 peppercorns
1 cup soft white
 breadcrumbs
15 g butter
pinch ground cloves

1 Remove any loose fat from chicken; thoroughly clean and dry the bird. Place rosemary sprigs, garlic and butter in cavity of prepared chicken.

2 Lay bacon rashers criss-cross over chicken breast. Secure bacon in several places with small skewers or with toothpicks.

3 Place chicken in a baking dish on a rack and brush with oil. Bake in a moderate oven 180°C for about 1½ hours, basting frequently with stock.

(Cover chicken with foil if necessary to prevent overbrowning of bacon.) Allow chicken to rest for 15 minutes before carving; keep it warm while making Bread Sauce.

4 To prepare Bread Sauce: Place onion, milk, bay leaf and peppercorns in a small pan, simmer for 15 minutes. Strain, stir in breadcrumbs, butter and cloves.

5 Add extra rosemary to pan juices from chicken, pour over chicken, serve immediately with the Bread Sauce.

HINT
Let poultry 'rest' for at least 15 minutes after roasting. This will make the meat, particularly the breast meat, more easy to carve. Put the bird on a heated platter and cover with foil to keep hot.

HINT
If you are buying a frozen chicken which you intend to keep stored in your freezer, make it the last item of purchase and transport it home as quickly as possible. If it is still frozen hard, it can go straight into your freezer without rewrapping. If it has started to thaw, you must place it in the refrigerator and allow it to thaw completely. Then cook it promptly, cool it quickly, wrap and freeze it. It is dangerous to re-freeze thawed, uncooked poultry. Food poisoning can result.

Coq au Vin

Coq au Vin

This popular dish is a tradition in French Provincial cooking and has become a favourite for both entertaining and family meals.

Preparation time:
  30 minutes
Cooking time:
  1 hour
Serves 4-6

2 teaspoons vegetable oil
1 large onion, chopped
2 cloves garlic, crushed
10 chicken thighs (or cut of choice), skinned

125 g leg ham, chopped
250 g small button mushrooms
2 cups red wine
2 tablespoons cornflour
2 tablespoons water
2 tablespoons chopped parsley

1 Heat oil in a large pan. Cook onion until softened. Add garlic and chicken. Cook chicken until lightly browned on all sides. Remove chicken from pan, set aside.
2 Add ham and mushrooms to pan. Cook 1 minute. Return chicken to pan with wine. Bring to the boil,

reduce heat. Simmer, covered, for 1 hour or until chicken is tender.
3 Blend cornflour with water until smooth. Gradually stir into wine sauce. Cook, stirring constantly, until the sauce boils and thickens. Simmer 3 minutes.
4 Add parsley just before serving. Serve with rice, salad and crusty bread.

Note: This dish can be made up to two days in advance and refrigerated if desired. The flavour develops beautifully.

19

Almond-crusted Chicken

Preparation time:
  30 minutes
Cooking time:
  40 minutes
Serves 4

1 x 1.2 kg chicken
1 egg, lightly beaten
½ cup chopped slivered
  almonds
2 cups grated Swiss
  cheese
¼ cup grated Parmesan
  cheese
¼ teaspoon sweet
  paprika

1 Cut legs and thighs from chicken in one whole piece. Cut through joint of each leg to make a total of 4 pieces.
2 Cut off wings leaving a small piece of breast meat attached. Wing tips can be removed and discarded if preferred (or use them to make chicken stock).
3 To remove breast, cut through rib bones along each side, close to the backbone. Cut breast into 4 equal pieces.
4 Dip chicken pieces in egg. Drain off excess. Coat with combined remaining ingredients, pressing them on firmly. Place in a lightly greased baking dish. Bake in a hot oven 200°C for 35-40 minutes or until cooked when tested. (See Note.) Serve with new potatoes and vegetables of your choice.

Note: It is important to ensure chicken is thoroughly cooked. Many cases of food poisoning result from eating insufficiently cooked chicken. Insert a skewer into the thickest part. If the juices run clear, the chicken is cooked; if they are still pink, it is not.

1. For Almond-crusted Chicken: Cut legs and thighs from bird in one whole piece.

2. Cut off wings. Leave a small piece of meat from breast attached.

Almond-crusted Chicken

3. *Cut through rib bones along each side, near backbone, and remove breast meat.*

4. *Coat pieces in beaten egg, then in combined almonds, cheeses and paprika.*

Chicken Parmigiana with Tomato Sauce

Preparation time:
  40 minutes
Cooking time:
  12 minutes
Serves 4

Tomato Sauce
1 tablespoon oil
1 onion, finely chopped
1 clove garlic, crushed
1 x 425 g can tomatoes, chopped
1/4 cup red wine
3 tablespoons tomato paste
1/2 teaspoon dried oregano
freshly ground black pepper

Chicken Parmigiana
1 egg
2 tablespoons milk
3/4 cup dry breadcrumbs
1/2 cup grated Parmesan cheese
4 chicken breast fillets, pounded until even
4 tablespoons olive oil

1 To prepare Sauce: Heat oil in a pan. Cook onion until tender. Stir in remaining ingredients. Bring to the boil, reduce heat, simmer uncovered for 15 minutes. Keep warm.
2 To prepare Chicken: Whisk together egg and milk in a shallow dish. Combine breadcrumbs and half the cheese on another plate.
3 Dip each chicken breast into the egg mixture. Press into breadcrumb mixture to coat. Refrigerate for 15 minutes.
4 Heat half the oil in a large, shallow pan. Cook 2 breasts until crisp and golden on both sides. Drain and wipe pan with absorbent paper, heat remaining oil. Cook remaining chicken. Drain.
5 Top chicken with Tomato Sauce and sprinkle with remaining Parmesan cheese. Serve with spaghetti and steamed zucchini.

Spanish-style Chicken Casserole

Preparation time:
  20 minutes
Cooking time:
  35 minutes
Serves 8

2 tablespoons oil
2 kg chicken pieces
freshly ground black pepper
2 onions, chopped
2 cloves garlic, crushed
2 red or green capsicum, seeded and cut into strips
6 slices prosciutto, chopped
1 x 425 g can peeled tomatoes
1/2 cup white wine
12 black olives
12 green olives

1 Heat oil in a large pan. Cook chicken a few pieces at a time, sprinkling them with pepper, until golden. Transfer to a plate.
2 Cook onion, garlic, capsicum and prosciutto for 5-8 minutes or until tender, but not browned.
3 Add chicken and undrained tomatoes, wine and olives. Simmer, uncovered, for 35 minutes or until tender. Serve casseroled chicken with steamed potatoes and green salad.

HINT

Coat chicken pieces for pan-frying in flour seasoned with your favourite herbs or spices. Alternatively, dip the pieces in beaten egg and coat with fresh or dry brown or white breadcrumbs mixed with grated cheese, finely chopped nuts, fresh herbs or spices, or a combination of these, pressed on firmly. If using nuts, cook the chicken over a gentle heat to prevent them burning and becoming bitter.

Chicken Stroganoff

Chicken Stroganoff

Preparation time:
  20 minutes
Cooking time:
  15 minutes
Serves 6

30 g butter
2 tablespoons oil
2 onions, thinly sliced
2 cloves garlic, crushed
8 chicken thigh fillets,
  sliced
250 g mushrooms, sliced
2 teaspoons sweet
  paprika
1 cup sour cream

¼ cup tomato paste
freshly ground black
  pepper
2 tablespoons chopped
  parsley

1 Heat butter and oil
together in a large
frying pan. Cook onion
and garlic until onion is
tender.
2 Add chicken pieces.
Cook, turning, until
chicken is tender. Stir in
mushrooms and
paprika. Cook until
tender.
3 Stir in combined sour
cream, tomato paste
and pepper. Simmer
gently until heated
through. Sprinkle with
parsley. Serve with
boiled rice or pasta.

HINT
After cooking a
casserole ahead of
time for reheating
that day, cool it
rapidly by immersing
the base of the dish
in iced water. Then
store it, covered, in
the refrigerator.
Harmful bacteria
will develop if it is
left to cool slowly at
room temperature.

Chicken Loaf in Sour Cream Pastry

Chicken Loaf in Sour Cream Pastry

Preparation time:
  45 minutes + 1 hour chilling
Cooking time:
  45 minutes
Serves 6

Pastry
2¹/2 cups plain flour
185 g butter, cut into small pieces
3 tablespoons sour cream
1 egg yolk
1 egg, lightly beaten, for glaze

Filling
60 g butter
1 large onion, finely chopped
1 kg chicken mince
2 tablespoons finely chopped chives
1 tablespoon fresh rosemary leaves
125 g button mushrooms, finely chopped
¹/2 cup chicken stock
freshly ground black pepper
¹/2 cup soft white breadcrumbs
2 extra eggs, beaten
³/4 cup grated Cheddar cheese
¹/4 cup finely chopped parsley

1 To prepare Pastry: Sift flour into bowl, rub in butter until mixture resembles fine breadcrumbs. Combine sour cream and egg yolk; mix into flour mixture to make a firm dough. Gently knead until smooth; wrap and chill at least 1 hour.

2 To prepare Filling: In a large pan, melt butter. Add onion and chicken mince, cook, stirring with a fork to break up any lumps. Add herbs, mushrooms, stock and pepper to taste. Cook and stir until boiling. Reduce heat, simmer uncovered until all liquid is absorbed, about 20 minutes. Stir in breadcrumbs; cool completely.
3 Combine extra eggs, cheese and parsley; stir into chicken mixture. Set aside.
4 On a lightly floured surface, roll out half the pastry to line base and sides of a lightly greased 28 x 18 cm shallow baking tray, leaving a short overhang. Press filling into tin, smoothing evenly. Glaze pastry edges with beaten egg.
5 Roll out about three-quarters of the remaining pastry and cover filling; trim and press edges together to seal. Brush with glaze. Roll remaining pastry into a rectangle; cut lengthwise into strips. Place in a criss-cross pattern over top of pie. Brush with glaze; pierce top to let steam escape.
6 Bake at 180°C until pastry is golden, 40-45 minutes. Cool slightly before serving; cut into slices.

Curried Yoghurt Chicken

Curried Yoghurt Chicken

Preparation time:
  20 minutes + 2 hours
  marinating
Cooking time:
  45 minutes
Serves 6

1 cup plain yoghurt
1/2 cup coconut cream
1/4 cup fresh coriander,
  chopped
1 onion, finely chopped
1 clove garlic, crushed
1 teaspoon finely grated
  lime rind
1 tablespoon lime juice
1 tablespoon curry
  powder
freshly ground black
  pepper
1 kg chicken pieces
1 cup plain yoghurt,
  extra

1 Combine yoghurt, coconut cream, coriander, onion, garlic, rind, juice and curry powder in a large, shallow glass or ceramic dish. Add chicken pieces. Mix to coat completely.
2 Cover with plastic wrap. Marinate for several hours or leave overnight in the refrigerator.
3 Remove chicken from marinade. Place on a baking tray. Bake in a moderate oven 180°C for 40-45 minutes.
4 Blend remaining marinade with extra yoghurt. Heat gently in a small pan. Season to taste. Serve chicken with sauce, rice and salad.

Chicken Chop Suey

1 *For Chicken Chop Suey: Stir-fry sliced chicken and pork mince in hot oil.*

2. *Stir-fry chopped vegetables and garlic for 3 minutes only to retain their crispness.*

Chicken Chop Suey

Preparation time:
  20 minutes
Cooking time:
  8 minutes
Serves 6

2 tablespoons oil
2 chicken breast fillets,
  thinly sliced
250 g pork mince
1/2 Chinese cabbage,
  shredded
4 stalks celery, sliced
2 carrots, chopped
2 onions, chopped
1 capsicum, seeded and
  chopped
1 clove garlic, crushed
1 cup chicken stock
1 tablespoon soy sauce
2 teaspoons cornflour
1 teaspoon ground
  ginger
1 x 190 g can
  champignons, drained
1 x 285 g can bamboo
  shoots, drained
1 x 227 g can water
  chestnuts, drained

1 Heat oil in wok or frying pan. Add chicken and pork mince. Stir-fry until chicken is cooked and mince is browned. Remove from pan.
2 Add cabbage, celery, carrot, onion, capsicum and garlic to wok. Stir-fry for 3 minutes.
3 Pour in combined stock, soy sauce, cornflour (dissolved in a little of the stock until smooth) and ginger. Stir-fry until sauce boils and thickens.
4 Return chicken and pork to pan with remaining ingredients. Stir-fry for 2-3 minutes. Serve with boiled rice or noodles.

Note: The secret to delicious, aromatic stir-fries is to keep the wok hot and stir constantly for fast, even cooking. Stir-frying retains all the natural flavours, textures and colours of food.

Cabbage Rolls filled with Chicken

Preparation time:
  35 minutes
Cooking time:
  1 hour
Serves 4

Filling
1 tablespoon olive oil
1 onion, finely chopped
125 g mushrooms,
  chopped
400 g chicken mince
1/2 cup cooked brown
  rice
freshly ground black
  pepper
1 egg white
8-10 whole cabbage
  leaves

Sauce
1 1/2 cups tomato purée
1/2 cup water
1/4 cup light sour
  cream
1 clove garlic, crushed
1/2 teaspoon sugar
pinch ground oregano

3. Add combined stock, soy sauce, cornflour and ground ginger.

4. Return chicken mixture and remaining vegetables to wok.

1 To prepare Filling: Heat oil in a large pan. Cook onion until tender. Stir in mushrooms and chicken mince. Cook until mince is browned, using a fork to break up any lumps. Cool. Drain off fat.

2 Transfer mince mixture to a large bowl. Add rice, pepper and egg white. Mix well. Set aside.

3 Blanch cabbage leaves by placing in boiling water for 1-2 minutes or until just tender. Cut away thick stalks. This will enable the leaves to be rolled without breaking. If leaves are very large, they may be cut in half.

4 To prepare Sauce: Combine all ingredients. Mix well. Set aside.

5 To assemble, place 1-2 tablespoons of filling (depending on size of leaf) on each leaf. Roll up as a parcel. Secure with toothpicks.

6 Arrange rolls in an ovenproof dish. Pack closely together. Pour sauce over rolls. Bake in a moderate oven 180°C for about 1 hour. Serve with steamed vegetables or salad.

Caribbean Chicken Casserole

Preparation time:
  20 minutes + 30 minutes marinating
Cooking time:
  45 minutes
Serves 4

1 x 1.5 kg chicken, jointed
2 teaspoons finely grated lemon rind
2 tablespoons lemon juice
1 tablespoon teriyaki sauce
freshly ground black pepper
2 tablespoons oil

1 onion, sliced
1 clove garlic, crushed
1 x 450 g can crushed pineapple
2 large tomatoes, peeled and chopped
1/3 cup raisins
1/4 cup desiccated coconut
1 tablespoon chopped coriander
1/4 teaspoon ground cinnamon
2 tablespoons water
1 tablespoon cornflour

1 Place chicken in a bowl with lemon rind and juice, teriyaki sauce and pepper. Mix well. Marinate about 30 minutes, stirring occasionally.

2 Heat oil in pan. Cook drained chicken on all sides until golden. Place in the base of a large casserole dish. Pour over remaining marinade.

3 Cook onion and garlic in remaining oil in pan. Spoon over

1. For Cabbage Rolls filled with Chicken: Blanch leaves briefly in boiling water.

2. Roll leaves around filling to make neat parcels. Secure them with toothpicks.

Roast Chicken with Parsley Stuffing

chicken. Spoon the combined pineapple, tomatoes, raisins, coconut, coriander and cinnamon over chicken.

4 Bake, covered, in a moderate oven 180°C for 45 minutes or until chicken is tender. Blend water and cornflour to make a smooth paste. Stir into casserole.

5 Bake, uncovered, for a further 10 minutes. Serve with rice.

Roast Chicken with Parsley Stuffing

Preparation time:
  35 minutes
Cooking time:
  1 hour
Serves 4

1 x 1.4 kg chicken
1 onion, chopped
1 clove garlic, crushed
30 g butter
1 cup parsley, chopped
1 cup fresh breadcrumbs
1 egg, lightly beaten
freshly ground black
  pepper

1 Remove any loose fat from chicken; clean and dry chicken thoroughly. Set aside. Cook onion and garlic in butter until golden.

2 Combine parsley and breadcrumbs, add onion mixture, egg and pepper. Loosen skin of chicken from breast. Push stuffing under skin.

3 Place chicken on a trivet in a roasting dish, pour about 1 cup of water into dish. Bake in a moderately hot oven 190°C for about 1 hour or until cooked. Serve carved with potatoes, baked pumpkin, carrots and peas.

Quick, smart solutions

Ease of preparation is one of the most important criteria for busy cooks. Chicken pieces – thighs, wings, breast fillets, drumsticks – are now readily available at chicken shops and supermarkets. Keep a supply on hand in the freezer. Purchase ready-cooked barbecued chickens as the basis for a meal when you need to cut down further on cooking time. You can make things even easier for yourself if you have a well-stocked pantry; sesame oil, bottled tomato sauce, soy, relishes, chutneys, ground herbs and spices, nuts and mustards, pita bread and pizza bases will lend flexibility to your cooking, helping you ring the changes time and again.

Chicken Pita Pizzas

Preparation time:
  15 minutes
Cooking time:
  15 minutes
Serves 6

6 rounds wholemeal
  Lebanese bread, about
  12 cm in diameter
1/4 cup tomato pickle or
  chutney
125 g cooked chicken,
  slivered
125 g fresh mushrooms,
  sliced
1 red or green
  capsicum, sliced

dried oregano or basil
  leaves
1 cup grated mozzarella
  cheese

1 Place bread rounds on baking tray. Spread tomato pickle evenly over each piece. Top with the sliced chicken, mushrooms and capsicum. Sprinkle with herb of your choice, then with grated mozzarella cheese.
2 Bake the bread rounds in a hot oven 200°C for 15 minutes, until chicken is cooked and cheese is bubbling. Serve immediately.

Chicken Pita Pizza,
Grilled Chicken
Pizzaiola (page 32)

Grilled Chicken Pizzaiola

Preparation time:
  20 minutes
Cooking time:
  8 minutes
Serves 4

1 tablespoon olive oil
1 large onion, finely
  chopped
2 cloves garlic, finely
  chopped
1 x 425 g can tomato
  pieces
1 teaspoon dried basil
  leaves
1 teaspoon dried
  oregano leaves
1 tablespoon drained
  capers
4 chicken breast fillets
a little extra olive oil

1 Heat oil in pan, add onion and garlic and cook, stirring, until tender. Add the tomatoes and herbs and cook, stirring, until boiling.
2 Reduce heat, simmer uncovered, stirring frequently until sauce is thickened, about 15 minutes. Stir in capers and keep warm.
3 Lightly brush chicken fillets with extra oil. Grill about 8 cm from heat until cooked, about 4 minutes for each side.
4 Place chicken on heated serving platter, pour over sauce. Serve immediately with salad and crusty bread.

Chicken with Walnuts and Blue Cheese

Preparation time:
  15 minutes
Cooking time:
  15 minutes
Serves 4

8 chicken thigh fillets,
  skinned
olive oil
3 medium tomatoes,
  thickly sliced
1/3 cup walnut pieces
6 spring onions, finely
  chopped
90 g blue vein cheese,
  crumbled

1 Brush chicken with oil; place under preheated grill and cook, turning frequently, until almost tender. Remove from the heat.
2 Scatter tomatoes in base of griller-proof dish. Grill for about 2 minutes, add chicken. Sprinkle with the walnuts, spring onion and cheese.
3 Continue grilling until chicken is tender and cheese is golden, 5-8 minutes more. Serve with sauté potatoes and steamed spinach.

Oriental Chicken Kebabs

Preparation time:
  30 minutes + 30
  minutes marinating
Cooking time:
  10 minutes
Serves 4

1 tablespoon light soy
  sauce
1 tablespoon white wine
2 teaspoons whole
  grain mustard

Oriental Chicken Kebabs

2 teaspoons snipped
  chives
1 teaspoon oil
1 clove garlic, crushed
1 teaspoon grated ginger
4 chicken breast fillets,
  cut into chunks
bamboo skewers,
  soaked in water
12 button mushrooms
12 cherry tomatoes
1 onion, cut into eighths
1 green capsicum,
  seeded and cubed
3 canned, unsweetened
  pineapple rings,
  quartered

1 Combine soy sauce, wine, mustard, chives, oil, garlic and ginger in a glass bowl. Add chicken. Marinate for 30 minutes, turning chicken frequently.
2 Thread chicken onto skewers, alternating meat with mushrooms, tomatoes, onion, capsicum and pineapple.
3 Grill kebabs for 5-10 minutes, turning and basting frequently. Serve with a salad.

HINT
Fresh chicken has a pleasant, very mild, fresh aroma. Should it have a slight odour, rinse it under cold water and rub it thoroughly with a cut lemon. Alternatively, make up a solution of vinegar and water and dip the chicken briefly in it. Do not store – cook at once.

1. For Chicken with Lemon and Coriander: Dust with seasoned flour.

2. After browning the chicken, add stock, lemon juice, coriander and garlic to pan.

Chicken with Lemon and Coriander

Chicken with Lemon and Coriander

Preparation time:
  25 minutes
Cooking time:
  20 minutes
Serves 4

1 x 1.2 kg chicken,
  quartered
2 tablespoons plain
  flour
freshly ground black
  pepper
2 tablespoons olive oil
½ cup chicken stock
2 tablespoons lemon
  juice
2 tablespoons chopped
  coriander
2 cloves garlic, crushed
1 tablespoon cream

1 Dust chicken pieces with combined flour and pepper. Shake off excess.
2 Heat oil in pan. Add chicken pieces. Cook on both sides until golden. Reduce heat.
3 Add chicken stock, lemon juice, coriander and garlic. Simmer chicken for 15-20 minutes or until cooked.
4 Remove chicken pieces from pan. Keep warm. Stir cream into pan. Boil quickly until slightly thickened. Serve chicken with sauce, noodles and a salad.

Chicken Chilli Pasta

Preparation time:
  20 minutes
Cooking time:
  25 minutes
Serves 6

2 teaspoons olive oil
1 onion, chopped
1 red or green
  capsicum, seeded and
  chopped
1 clove garlic, crushed

3. *Remove chicken from pan; stir cream into the pan juices.*

4. *Bring cream and pan juices quickly to the boil and cook until slightly thickened.*

35

n chopped
1 teaspoon chilli sauce
500 g chicken mince
1 x 425 g can tomato
  pieces
1 cup white wine or
  water
½ teaspoon dried
  oregano
½ teaspoon dried basil
freshly ground black
  pepper
500 g pasta of your
  choice
2 tablespoons parsley,
  chopped

1 Heat oil in a large
pan. Cook onion,
capsicum and garlic
until onion is tender.
Stir in chopped chilli
and chilli sauce.
2 Add chicken mince.
Cook, breaking mince
up with a fork, until
chicken changes colour.
3 Mix in tomatoes,
wine, oregano, basil
and pepper. Simmer,
uncovered, for 15
minutes, stirring
occasionally.
4 Cook pasta in plenty
of boiling water until
just tender. Drain. Stir
parsley through sauce.
Serve over pasta. Serve
freshly grated Parmesan
cheese and crusty garlic
bread with this dish.

Marinated Taco Chicken

Marinated Taco Chicken

Preparation time:
  15 minutes + 30
  minutes marinating
Cooking time:
  15 minutes
Serves 6

⅔ cup bottled, chunky,
  medium-hot taco sauce
¼ cup Dijon mustard
2 tablespoons lemon
  juice
6 chicken breast fillets
30 g butter
¼ cup sour cream
chopped parsley
green salad and corn
  chips, for serving

1 Combine taco sauce,
mustard and lemon
juice in shallow glass or
ceramic dish. Add
chicken, turning to
coat. Cover and
marinate for 30 minutes
or overnight in the
refrigerator.
2 Melt butter in large
pan until foaming.
Drain chicken,
reserving marinade.
Cook breasts until
browned, turning them
once, about 5 minutes
each side.
3 Add reserved
marinade. Simmer,
uncovered, 5 minutes
more. Remove chicken
to a platter, using a
slotted spoon. Simmer
marinade until
thickened, serve with
chicken.
4 Top each breast
with a spoonful of sour
cream and garnish with
chopped parsley. Serve
with green salad and
corn chips.

Chilli Tomato Chicken

Preparation time:
  15 minutes
Cooking time:
  10 minutes
Serves 6

30 g butter
2 tablespoons oil
6 chicken breast fillets
1 avocado, peeled and
  sliced
3 tomatoes, thickly
  sliced
2 cups grated Cheddar
  cheese

Chilli Sauce
1 clove garlic, crushed
1 cup tomato purée
1 tablespoon chilli sauce
1 teaspoon chopped chilli
few drops Tabasco sauce
freshly ground black
  pepper
1/4 teaspoon dried
  oregano
1 teaspoon brown sugar

1 Heat butter and oil in a large pan. Add chicken and cook for 3-5 minutes each side or until tender and golden. Place in a shallow ovenproof dish.
2 Top with avocado, tomato and cheese. Bake in a moderate oven 180°C for 5 minutes or until cheese has melted.
3 To prepare Chilli Sauce: Remove all but a teaspoon of fat from pan. Cook garlic until lightly golden. Stir in purée, chilli sauce, chilli, Tabasco, pepper, oregano and brown sugar. Bring to the boil, reduce heat, simmer uncovered for 3-5 minutes.
4 Serve chicken with Chilli Sauce and vegetables of your choice.

Chilli Tomato Chicken

Tuscan Chicken

Tuscan Chicken

Preparation time:
  20 minutes
Cooking time:
  15 minutes
Serves 4

60 g butter
4 chicken breast fillets, cut in 2 cm cubes
2 tablespoons brandy
1 x 250 g punnet cherry tomatoes
250 g button mushrooms, sliced
1 cup dry white wine or chicken stock
freshly ground black pepper
dried rosemary leaves, crushed
chopped parsley, for garnish

1 In large pan, melt butter until foaming. Add chicken pieces and cook until white, turning them occasionally, about 4 minutes.
2 Add brandy, then tomatoes and mushrooms. Cook and stir for 3 minutes. Add wine or stock, pepper and rosemary to taste.
3 Simmer, uncovered, until liquid is reduced and mixture is slightly thickened. Sprinkle with parsley to serve.

Stir-fried Chicken with Pineap...

Stir-fried Chicken with Pineapple

Preparation time:
  15 minutes
Cooking time:
  10 minutes
Serves 4

30 g butter
1/2 cup whole or
  slivered blanched
  almonds
1 tablespoon oil
3 chicken breast fillets,
  sliced
1 tablespoon chopped
  mint
1 red capsicum, seeded
  and sliced

1 x 450 g can pineapple
  pieces, drained and
  juice reserved
2 stalks celery, sliced
2 tablespoons orange
  marmalade

1 Melt butter in a wok.
Stir-fry the almonds
until golden. Remove to
a plate.
2 Add oil to wok.
Stir-fry the chicken and
mint for 3-4 minutes or
until chicken is cooked.
3 Stir in capsicum,
pineapple and celery.
Blend marmalade with
reserved pineapple
juice. Pour into wok.
Heat through until
marmalade melts.
4 Return almonds to
wok. Toss ingredients
together. Serve
immediately with rice.

HINT
Keep uncooked chicken in the coldest part of the
refrigerator and cook within two days of
purchase. Whole chickens should be removed
from their wrappings, washed, patted dry and
jointed, if wished. Wrap the pieces again in clean
plastic wrap or foil and store in the fridge.

au Gratin

Chicken Broccoli au Gratin

Preparation time:
 15 minutes
Cooking time:
 30 minutes
Serves 6

*1 x 1.4 kg chicken,
 cooked and cooled*
*250 g broccoli, cut into
 florets*
*1 x 440 g can cream of
 chicken soup*
*4 spring onions, finely
 chopped*
*1 teaspoon curry
 powder*
*1 cup sour cream
freshly ground black
 pepper*
*1/4 cup grated Cheddar
 cheese*
*1/4 teaspoon sweet
 paprika*

1 Remove chicken meat from carcass. Cut into large pieces.
2 Cook broccoli in boiling water for 1-2 minutes. Drain. Refresh in cold water.
3 Combine chicken soup, spring onion, curry powder, sour cream and pepper in a bowl. Place the broccoli in a large, greased casserole dish. Top with the chicken.
4 Pour over soup mixture. Sprinkle with cheese and paprika.
5 Bake in a moderate oven 180°C for 30-40 minutes or until golden brown. Serve with boiled rice.

Note: A barbecued chicken may be used for this recipe. Alternatively, poach segmented chicken (or breasts) in a mixture of water and white wine in a moderate oven 180°C. Retain poaching liquid and use as the basis for a soup.

Italian-style Chicken

Preparation time:
  10 minutes
Cooking time:
  10 minutes
Serves 4

1 tablespoon olive oil
1 clove garlic, crushed
½ teaspoon dried thyme
½ teaspoon dried
  oregano

1 x 425 g can tomatoes
¼ cup dry white wine
¼ cup pitted black
  olives, quartered
1 barbecued chicken,
  skin removed and
  flesh cut into pieces

1 Heat oil in frying pan. Add garlic and herbs, cook gently for 30 seconds.
2 Add tomatoes and wine to pan. Bring to the boil, stirring occasionally. Cook until sauce has thickened.
3 Stir in olives and chicken. Cook for 1 minute. Serve immediately with hot pasta of your choice.

HINT
Scrub kitchen boards thoroughly in very hot water to remove all traces of chicken meat. A kitchen board is a breeding ground for bacteria.

Italian-style Chicken

Sizzling barbecues

Clockwise from top left: Teriyaki Kebabs, Tarragon Lemon Chicken (page 44), Cranberry Wings

The appeal of food cooked in the open air never wanes. For impromptu meals or large gatherings, the barbecue has no peers when it comes to preparing fast, flavoursome and nutritious meals. If you have no barbecue, the griller on your oven can produce excellent results, too. For kebabs, individual joints of poultry and whole spatchcock, marinades have a key role to play. The various flavours permeate the flesh and the acid content such as lemon juice, wine or vinegar, increases its tenderness. For thicker cuts, slash the flesh in several places to allow the flavours to be better absorbed. Baste the meat with the marinade occasionally during cooking to prevent it drying out.

Cranberry Wings

Preparation time:
  20 minutes + 2 hours
  marinating
Cooking time:
  30 minutes
Serves 6

1.5 kg chicken wings
freshly ground black
  pepper
3/4 cup orange
  marmalade
1/2 cup bottled
  cranberry sauce
1/2 cup spicy red
  barbecue sauce
1/3 cup white vinegar

1 In a glass or ceramic container, combine chicken wings, pepper, marmalade, cranberry sauce, barbecue sauce and vinegar. Stir to coat the chicken wings in the sauce mixture. Refrigerate, covered, for about 2 hours or leave overnight.
2 Barbecue or grill wings about 15 cm from heat, turning them occasionally, for 15-20 minutes. Continue cooking, basting wings with sauce mixture until cooked through and well glazed, about 10 minutes more.

Note: Wings can also be cooked in a moderate oven 180°C for about 40 minutes. After marinating, place drained wings in a baking dish with a little water, cover, bake, brushing with marinade occasionally during cooking. Uncover for the final 10 minutes or so, cooking until crisp and golden.

Teriyaki Kebabs

Preparation time:
 20 minutes + 1 hour
 marinating
Cooking time:
 12 minutes
Serves 4

¼ *cup soy sauce*
¼ *cup oil*
¼ *cup dry sherry*
2 *cloves garlic, crushed*
2 *tablespoons brown sugar*
2 *teaspoons grated orange rind*
2 *teaspoons grated ginger*
4 *chicken breast fillets, cut into 2.5 cm cubes*

1 Combine soy sauce, oil, sherry, garlic, sugar, orange rind and ginger. Place chicken in a shallow glass or ceramic container, pour marinade over. Refrigerate for 1 hour or overnight, covered.

2 Thread chicken cubes onto greased metal or bamboo skewers. (Soak bamboo skewers in water for 30 minutes before use to prevent them burning.) Barbecue or grill kebabs about 15 cm from heat until tender, turning and basting them with the marinade, about 12 minutes.

Tarragon Lemon Chicken

Mix any selection of your favourite herbs and spices with the butter and use for basting. This chicken dish is delicious served hot or cold.

Preparation time:
 20 minutes
Cooking time:
 20 minutes
Serves 4

90 g *unsalted butter*
2 *tablespoons finely chopped chives*
1 *tablespoon finely chopped fresh coriander*
1 *tablespoon lemon juice*
½ *teaspoon dried tarragon leaves*
¼ *teaspoon paprika*
8 *chicken thigh fillets*
freshly ground pepper

1 Place butter in small pan over a low heat, stirring until melted, add the chives, coriander, lemon juice, tarragon and paprika.

2 Sprinkle chicken with pepper. Barbecue or grill slowly until tender and golden, turning and basting frequently with butter mixture, about 15-20 minutes. Serve chicken with seasonal salad and potatoes.

Marinated Wings

Preparation time:
 20 minutes +
 overnight marinating
Cooking time:
 30 minutes
Serves 6

1 kg *chicken wings*

Marinade
1 *onion, finely chopped*
¼ *cup sour cream*
2 *tablespoons oil*
2 *tablespoons lemon juice*
1 *tablespoon honey*
1 *tablespoon soy sauce*
2 *teaspoons grated lemon rind*
1 *teaspoon dried basil*
freshly ground black pepper

1 Place chicken in a shallow glass or ceramic dish. Combine onion, sour cream, oil, juice, honey, soy, lemon rind, basil and pepper.

Barbecued Chicken Burgers

Pour over the chicken, cover. Marinate overnight in refrigerator.
2 Barbecue or grill chicken, turning occasionally, for about 20-25 minutes.

Barbecued Chicken Burgers

Preparation time:
30 minutes
Cooking time:
12 minutes
Serves 4

350 g chicken mince
4 spring onions, finely chopped
2 tablespoons fresh breadcrumbs
¼ teaspoon dried basil
2 tablespoons oil
2 rashers rindless bacon, halved
1 avocado, sliced

1 Combine chicken mince, spring onions, breadcrumbs and basil. Divide into 4 equal portions. Shape into patties.
2 Cook burgers over a preheated, oiled barbecue grill for about 10-12 minutes. Grill bacon until crisp. Drain on absorbent paper.
3 Serve on a toasted hamburger bun with avocado slices.

Serving variation: These burgers can be 'custom-made' to your family's taste. Add other fillings such as sliced beetroot, fried egg, fried mushrooms or tomato, and barbecue or chilli sauce.

Spatchcocks with Lemon, Sesame and Coriander,
Oriental Chicken Maryland (page 48)

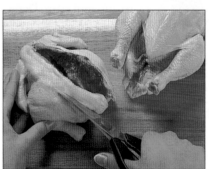

1. For Spatchcocks: Use sharp kitchen scissors to cut away the backbone.

2. Press firmly and flatten spatchcocks prior to marinating.

Spatchcocks with Lemon, Sesame and Coriander

Preparation time:
  20 minutes +
  overnight marinating
Cooking time:
  30 minutes
Serves 6

4 small spatchcocks
2 tablespoons olive oil
2 teaspoons sesame oil
1/2 cup lemon juice
1 tablespoon coriander
  seeds, crushed
2 cloves garlic, crushed
shredded lemon rind
lemon slices, to garnish

1 Throughly clean and dry spatchcocks. Use kitchen scissors or shears to cut along one side of the backbone. Then cut along the other side and discard backbone. Flatten each spatchcock slightly.

2 Combine oils, lemon juice, coriander seeds and garlic, mix well. Place spatchcocks in a shallow glass or ceramic dish, pour over marinade. Cover and refrigerate overnight, turning occasionally.
3 Remove spatchcocks from marinade, barbecue or grill about 12 cm from heat for about 30 minutes, basting occasionally. Serve hot or cold sprinkled with lemon rind. Garnish with lemon slices.

HINT
A spatchcock is a chicken of about six weeks of age. It weighs about 500 g and may be labelled a size 5. A chicken for roasting is under six months old, while one for boiling could be 18 months old or more.

3. Crush coriander seeds and add to oils, lemon juice and garlic.

4. Place spatchcocks in a glass dish and pour the marinade over them.

Devilled Chicken

Preparation time:
  25 minutes + 1 hour
  marinating
Cooking time:
  25 minutes
Serves 4

1 tomato, peeled and
  finely chopped
1/2 cup tomato sauce
2 tablespoons red wine
1 tablespoon olive oil
1 tablespoon tomato
  paste
2 teaspoons
  Worcestershire sauce
1/4 teaspoon mixed
  dried herbs
few drops Tabasco sauce
4 chicken Marylands

1 Combine tomato,
tomato sauce, wine, oil,
tomato paste,
Worcestershire sauce,
herbs and Tabasco, mix
well. Slash chicken
through thicker parts
with a small, sharp
knife. Place in shallow
glass or ceramic bowl,
marinate in the sauce
for 1 hour or longer,
basting frequently.

2 Barbecue or grill
chicken, turning and
basting with marinade
until it is cooked
through, about 25
minutes. Serve with
salad and crusty bread.

Oriental Chicken Maryland

Preparation time:
  20 minutes + 1 hour
  marinating
Cooking time:
  25 minutes
Serves 4

1/2 cup soy sauce
1/4 cup honey
2 tablespoons sesame
  seeds
2 teaspoons sesame oil
1/2 teaspoon ground
  ginger
2 cloves garlic, crushed
4 chicken Marylands

1 Combine soy sauce,
honey, sesame seeds,
oil, ginger and garlic in
a shallow glass or
ceramic dish. Slash
chicken through thicker
parts with a small,
sharp knife. Add

chicken pieces to the
marinade. Cover
completely with the
mixture. Allow to
marinate for 1 hour or
longer, basting chicken
frequently.

2 Barbecue or grill
chicken, turning and
basting with marinade,
until cooked right
through. Serve with a
rice salad.

Barbecued Satay Chicken

Preparation time:
  20 minutes + 30
  minutes marinating
Cooking time:
  12 minutes
Serves 4

6 chicken thigh fillets,
  cut into 2.5 cm cubes
8 skewers (see Note)
1/3 cup crunchy peanut
  butter
1 clove garlic, crushed
1 tablespoon oil
2 teaspoons soy sauce
pinch chilli powder

1 Thread the chicken
pieces onto skewers.
Place in a shallow dish.
Combine peanut butter,
garlic, oil, soy sauce
and chilli powder, mix
well. Pour over chicken,
marinate for 30 minutes
at room temperature.

2 Barbecue or grill
for 10-12 minutes or
until cooked.

HINT

Appearances are important. The flesh of a fresh
chicken should be moist, with no dry spots. The
breast should be plump. If blood or juices are
visible in the bottom of the plastic packaging, it
indicates that the chickens have been in the
display cabinet for longer than is ideal. If these
are offered on special, cook them the same day.

Barbecued Satay Chicken

Serve with a crisp green salad or with rice.

Note: If using bamboo skewers, first soak them in water for 30 minutes to prevent them burning when the food is cooked.

HINT
Once chicken has been cooked, it should be stored in the coldest part of the refrigerator and eaten within two or three days. If there is any stuffing, remove it and store it separately in a covered container; it can be reheated in a moderate oven for about 30 minutes. Gravy and broth must also be stored in separate containers.

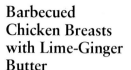

Barbecued Chicken Breasts with Lime-Ginger Butter

Preparation time:
  20 minutes + 30
  minutes chilling
Cooking time:
  25 minutes
Serves 6

185g unsalted butter
1 teaspoon finely grated
  lime rind
2 tablespoons lime
  juice
2 teaspoons finely
  grated ginger
1 spring onion, finely
  chopped
1/2 cup parsley, finely
  chopped
6 chicken breast fillets
plain flour, for coating
  chicken

1 Beat butter with an electric mixer until light and fluffy. Add rind, juice, ginger and spring onion, mix until combined.
2 Shape mixture into a log about 4 cm in diameter and about 10 cm long. Wrap in greaseproof paper and chill 30 minutes. Roll log in parsley to coat, rewrap and chill until it is needed.
3 Dust chicken lightly with flour, barbecue over a preheated, oiled barbecue grill for about 20-25 minutes, turning occasionally, until chicken is just tender.
4 Cut chilled lime-ginger butter crosswise into 5 mm slices. Place 2 slices on top of each breast, and serve. The flavoured butter will melt to a delicious sauce.

Note: This dish is good served with herbed or saffron rice.

HINT
Flavoured butters are one of the quickest and easiest ways to 'dress up' a simple barbecue. Use lemon juice, fresh herbs or spices of your choice.

Chicken Parcels with Honey Mustard Glaze

Preparation time:
  35 minutes
Cooking time:
  20-25 minutes
Serves 6-8

8 chicken thigh fillets
16 pitted prunes
8 spring onions, halved
2 tablespoons flaked
  almonds
4 rashers rindless
  bacon, halved
  lengthwise

Honey Mustard Glaze
1 tablespoon brown
  sugar
1 tablespoon Dijon
  mustard
1 tablespoon honey
15 g butter, melted
freshly ground black
  pepper

1 Open out each thigh fillet and place 2 prunes, 2 pieces of spring onion and a few flaked almonds on each one.
2 Roll up fillets, wrap a piece of bacon around each one. Secure with toothpicks.
3 Barbecue or grill over a low heat until cooked, about 20 minutes. Baste frequently with glaze.
4 To prepare Honey Mustard Glaze: Blend all ingredients together in a small bowl.

Note: Breast fillets can replace thighs in this recipe; reduce cooking time by 5 minutes.

HINT
Many combinations of ingredient can be used in a glaze. For a Ginger Honey Glaze, combine 1/2 cup soy sauce, 1/3 cup honey and 2 teaspoons ground ginger in a small pan. Bring mixture to the boil, stirring constantly. Makes about 3/4 cup.

*Chicken Parcels
with Honey
Mustard Glaze*

Special events

The most enjoyable occasions in our lives frequently revolve around eating. Birthdays, anniversaries and reunions demand food that complements the occasion and conjures happy memories for years to come. None of the recipes given here is difficult (although you may need a little more time to prepare them); their 'special' quality is achieved by the ingredients used – things slightly out of the ordinary that make them a cut above the rest. Dried fruits, blue cheese, spices, choux pastry and an array of shellfish combine wonderfully well with your trusty chicken pieces, spatchcock and larger birds.

Chicken with Olives, Apricots and Figs

Preparation time:
  30 minutes +
  overnight marinating
Cooking time:
  1¼ hours
Serves 6

½ cup dried figs
½ cup dried apricots
½ cup pitted black olives
¼ cup red wine vinegar
2 tablespoons olive oil
3 cloves garlic, crushed

1½ teaspoons dried thyme leaves
1 teaspoon ground cumin
½ teaspoon ground ginger
freshly ground black pepper
1.5 kg small chicken pieces
¼ cup red wine or orange juice
1 tablespoon packed brown sugar
thin strips of orange peel and fresh thyme, for garnish

1 In a large glass bowl, combine fruit, olives, vinegar, oil, garlic,

*Indonesian Chicken (page 54),
Chicken with Olives,
Apricots and Figs*

thyme and spices.

2 Discard any fat (and skin, if desired); add chicken to mixture. Cover and refrigerate overnight, turning the chicken occasionally.

3 Transfer mixture to a large, shallow baking dish. Combine wine and sugar; pour over chicken. Cover, bake in a moderately slow oven 160°C for 30 minutes.

4 Uncover; continue baking, basting frequently with cooking juices until chicken is tender, 45-50 minutes more.

5 With slotted spoon, transfer chicken to heated serving platter; spoon the figs and apricots and the olives over, sprinkle with orange peel and garnish with fresh thyme.

HINT

A 'dry' marinade consists of herbs and spices rubbed onto the meat; a 'wet' one may include oils, vinegars and lemon juice and is poured over the meat.

Indonesian Chicken

Preparation time:
  20 minutes + 2 hours marinating
Cooking time:
  20 minutes
Serves 6-8

1.5 kg chicken thighs
3 cloves garlic, crushed
1 teaspoon brown sugar
1 teaspoon ground black pepper
2 teaspoons ground coriander
1 teaspoon ground cumin
1 teaspoon ground turmeric
3 tablespoons tamarind pulp
oil, for shallow frying

1 Trim the thighs of excess fat and any tail pieces. Wash and dry well on absorbent paper.

2 Combine garlic with sugar, spices and tamarind pulp. Rub well over chicken pieces, cover and marinate overnight in the refrigerator, or for at least 2 hours at

---

HINT

Packaged stuffing mixes are useful when you're in a hurry. Use them as the basis for your own 'creation', stirring in 1 tablespoon grated orange rind, 1 teaspoon lemon rind, 1/4 cup chopped parsley, 1/4 cup finely chopped nuts of your choice or 2 tablespoons chopped celery leaves.

---

room temperature.

3 Heat enough oil to cover base of a large, heavy pan and cook the chicken pieces slowly over a medium heat, turning them with tongs to ensure they are an even golden brown all over. Drain on absorbent paper and serve warm with rice.

Chicken with Blue Cheese

Preparation time:
  30 minutes + 30 minutes chilling
Cooking time:
  5 minutes
Serves 4

4 chicken breast fillets, pounded to an even thickness
1 tablespoon chopped parsley
1 tablespoon chopped chives
100 g blue cheese (see Note)
1/4 cup plain flour
freshly ground black pepper
1 egg, lightly beaten
1/2 cup dry breadcrumbs
oil, for deep frying

1 Lay chicken breasts on a board. Sprinkle each with the parsley and chives. Divide cheese into 4 pieces. Place a piece of cheese on each chicken breast.

Tandoori-style Chicken

Roll up chicken. Secure each piece with toothpicks if necessary.
2 Dust chicken with combined flour and black pepper. Shake off excess. Dip into beaten egg. Coat with breadcrumbs, pressing firmly. Refrigerate for 30 minutes.
3 Heat oil in a large pan. Add chicken. Deep-fry for 5 minutes or until golden. Drain on absorbent paper. Serve with steamed vegetables.

Note: Brie may be substituted for blue cheese, if preferred.

Tandoori-style Chicken

Tandoori chicken is traditionally red in colour. Powdered food colouring may be added to the marinade to achieve this appearance.

Preparation time:
  20 minutes +
  overnight marinating
Cooking time:
  20 minutes
Serves 4

1 cup low-fat, plain yoghurt
1 onion, finely chopped

1 tablespoon finely grated lemon rind
2 tablespoons lemon juice
1 clove garlic, crushed
1 teaspoon ground coriander
1/2 teaspoon finely chopped fresh ginger
1/2 teaspoon ground cumin
1/4 teaspoon garam masala
4 chicken breast fillets

1 Combine all the ingredients except chicken in a glass or ceramic bowl.
2 Cut each chicken fillet into 8 pieces. Add to marinade. Mix well.

Roast Chicken in Cider

Cover with plastic wrap. Refrigerate overnight.

3 Remove chicken pieces from marinade with tongs, allowing excess marinade to drip off. Place chicken on a lightly oiled rack in a baking dish.

4 Bake in a very hot oven 220°C for 15-20 minutes or until cooked. Serve with boiled Basmati rice, pappadams and sambals (see Note).

Note: Sambals are side dishes such as tomato and onion, cucumber and yoghurt, banana and coconut, and mango chutney. Serve several with a curry. They complement rich, spicy foods.

HINT
Do not stuff poultry until you are about to roast the bird. The stuffing may spoil if left sitting inside the chicken for more than 15 minutes at room temperature. Make stuffing ahead and keep it in the refrigerator until you're ready to use it.

Roast Chicken in Cider

Preparation time:
35 minutes
Cooking time:
1¾ hours
Serves 4

4 rashers bacon, rind removed, cut into thin strips
1 x 1.3 kg chicken
60 g butter
1 white onion, cut into thin wedges
1 cup dry cider
1 cup chicken stock
2 bay leaves

*½ teaspoon dried
thyme leaves*
freshly ground pepper
6 medium carrots
4 medium potatoes
chopped parsley

1 Cook bacon in large, shallow pan until lightly golden. Transfer with slotted spoon to a shallow baking dish.
2 Wipe chicken dry. Fold back wings and tie legs together. Add butter to the bacon fat in pan and brown chicken slowly on all sides. Place chicken on top of bacon in dish.
3 Cook onion in pan juices until tender. Scatter over the chicken. Add cider, stock, bay leaves, thyme and pepper to chicken.
4 Place dish in oven and bake, uncovered, at 180°C for 30 minutes.
5 While chicken is cooking, peel carrots and potatoes. Cut into chunks and round off sharp edges to make neat shapes. Add the vegetable pieces to the chicken.
6 Continue baking, basting frequently with juices, until chicken and vegetables are tender, 1-1¼ hours more (see Note). Turn vegetables occasionally. Sprinkle with parsley. Cut the chicken into quarters and serve it with the vegetables.

Note: If chicken browns too quickly, cover lightly with a tent of aluminium foil.

Chicken Curry with Cashews and Almonds

Preparation time:
  30 minutes
Cooking time:
  50 minutes
Serves 6-8

⅓ cup oil
*3 large onions, finely
  chopped*
4 cloves garlic, crushed
*3 teaspoons finely
  chopped fresh ginger*
*2 tablespoons garam
  masala*
*1 tablespoon ground
  coriander*
1 teaspoon turmeric
1 x 425 g can tomatoes
*1.2 kg chicken pieces,
  skinned*
*1 tablespoon mint,
  finely chopped*
½ cup plain yoghurt
*½ cup unsalted cashew
  nuts*
*½ cup almonds,
  roughly chopped*

1 Heat oil in a large pan. Add onions. Cook until golden brown. Add garlic and ginger. Cook for 2 minutes.
2 Add garam masala, coriander and turmeric. Stir constantly over heat for 2 minutes.
3 Stir in undrained tomatoes. Add chicken pieces and mint. Cook over a low heat for about 45 minutes or until chicken is cooked. Stir occasionally to prevent sticking. Add a little water if sticking occurs.
4 Stir in yoghurt and nuts. Serve garnished with coriander.

HINT
Roast chicken with a delicious stuffing is a lovely treat, but the stuffing does have a tendency to spill out during cooking. Prevent this happening by simply placing a lightly buttered crust or slice of day-old bread rubbed with onion or garlic into the cavity opening.

HINT
Make your own garam masala by dry-roasting coriander, cumin and cardamom seeds, black peppercorns and cinnamon sticks separately until they release their fragrance. Grind them finely in an electric blender and store in an airtight container; keeps well for many months.

Chicken and Broccoli Gougère

Preparation time:
  40 minutes
Cooking time:
  30 minutes
Serves 6

2 large chicken breast
  fillets
1 x 250 g packet frozen
  broccoli pieces
1 cup grated Cheddar
  cheese
3 tablespoons cornflour
1 cup milk
freshly ground black
  pepper
1 cup water
75 g butter
1 cup plain flour
3 eggs

1 Cook chicken breasts
in simmering water to
cover for about 12
minutes, or until tender,
drain and cool. Cut into
strips. Cook broccoli in
boiling water until just
tender, drain thoroughly.
2 Combine cheese and
cornflour. Heat milk in
a pan until simmering.
Gradually add cheese
mixture, stirring
constantly, allowing
cheese to melt between
each addition. Season
with pepper, add
chicken and broccoli.
3 Put the water and
butter into a small
saucepan and bring to
the boil. Remove from

*Chicken Curry with Cashews and
Almonds (page 57), Chicken and Broccoli Gougère*

the heat and add flour all at once; beat vigorously, making sure the flour is thoroughly incorporated. Return to the heat and stir until mixture is smooth and comes away from the sides of the pan, cool slightly.

4 Add eggs, one at a time, beating well after each addition until they are thoroughly incorporated. Spread the mixture round the sides of a greased 25 cm dish, leaving a hollow in the centre. Pour the prepared cheese, chicken and broccoli filling into the hollow and bake in a hot oven 200°C for 30 minutes; the pastry rim will puff up. Serve at once with a seasonal salad.

Roast Spiced Spatchcock

Preparation time:
30 minutes
Cooking time:
40 minutes
Serves 6

3 medium-size
  spatchcocks
3 tablespoons honey
1 tablespoon
  rosewater
2 teaspoons ground
  cardamom
1 tablespoon lemon
  juice
2 tablespoons oil
1 teaspoon salt
good pinch cayenne
1/2 cup blanched
  almonds
coriander sprigs, for
  garnish

1 Pat spatchcocks dry with absorbent paper. Combine all other ingredients except almonds and coriander in a bowl.

2 Line a baking dish with a piece of foil large enough to wrap around the birds. Place spatchcocks on foil and pour a little honey mixture in each cavity. Pour remainder over spatchcocks and sprinkle with almonds, pressing them on.

3 Bring foil up around chicken and seal by folding over the edges. Bake in a moderate oven for 1 hour. Unwrap foil and spoon cooking juices over spatchcocks.

4 Roast, uncovered, for another 30 minutes, turning spatchcocks occasionally and basting again with juices. They should be golden brown at end of cooking time. Allow to rest for 5 minutes before carving. Garnish with coriander.

Roast Spiced Spatchcock

HINT
In hot weather, nuts quickly turn rancid. Buy them in small amounts as and when you need them for cooking, and keep them stored in an airtight container in a cool place.

Pecan Chicken

Pecan Chicken

Preparation time:
  30 minutes
Cooking time:
  10 minutes
Serves 4

4 chicken breast fillets
1 cup pecan halves
1/2 cup grated Gouda
  cheese
1/2 cup dry breadcrumbs
1/2 cup fresh white
  breadcrumbs
1 teaspoon ground sage
freshly ground black
  pepper
1 egg, lightly beaten
1 tablespoon water
60 g butter
2 tablespoons oil
sprigs of watercress or
  parsley, for garnish

1 Pound the fillets flat between sheets of plastic wrap to 1 cm thickness.
2 Reserve 8 pecan halves; finely chop remainder. In a shallow bowl, mix chopped pecans, cheese, breadcrumbs, sage and pepper to taste. In separate shallow bowl, beat egg and water until combined.
3 Coat fillets with half of the pecan mixture, dip them into the egg mixture, then coat with the remaining pecan mixture.
4 Heat butter and oil in large, shallow pan. Place fillets, 2 at a time, in pan; cook until golden brown and tender, turning once, 2-3 minutes per side. (Keep fillets warm while cooking the remainder.) Serve garnished with reserved pecans and watercress or parsley.

HINT
Fresh giblets – gizzard, heart, neck and liver – quickly deteriorate and should be cooked within 24 hours of purchase. Chicken livers make excellent pâté; they are available in tubs or can be purchased by the kilo from your butcher. The other giblets are very flavoursome and can be used to make soups and stocks.

Spanish Paella

Golden rice, seafood and chicken are baked in a rich broth in one of Spain's greatest special-occasion dishes.

Preparation time:
 40 minutes
Cooking time:
 1 hour
Serves 4

1 x 1.3 kg chicken, jointed
2 cloves garlic, finely chopped
1 tablespoon olive oil
1 medium onion, chopped
1¼ cups long-grain rice
6 threads saffron
3¼ cups chicken stock
375 g green prawns, peeled and deveined
2 red capsicum, seeded, cut into 2.5 cm squares
1½ cups frozen peas
12-16 small mussels on the shell
water or dry white wine

1 In large flame- and ovenproof casserole, cook chicken pieces and garlic in the oil. Remove to a plate and reserve.
2 Cook onion in drippings in pan until soft. Add rice; stir until golden. Add saffron and chicken stock, heat until boiling. Return chicken and garlic to casserole. Cover.
3 Bake in a moderately hot oven 190°C for 45 minutes. Add peeled prawns, red capsicum and frozen peas. Continue baking, covered, until the rice is tender and liquid absorbed, about 15 minutes or more.
4 Meanwhile, scrub mussels; place in deep pan with a splash of water or wine. Cover; simmer briskly until shells open. Discard any unopened shells.
5 To serve, fluff rice with a fork and top with mussels.

1. For Spanish Paella: Cook chicken pieces in oil and garlic.

2. Cook onion and rice in pan juices until onion is soft and rice golden.

Spanish Paella

3. Add the saffron threads and chicken stock and bring to the boil.

4. Scrub the mussels thoroughly, removing any beards, before cooking.

Index